MARRIAGE

To Have and To Hold

JUNE HUNT

AspirePress

Torrance, California

R🌹SE
PUBLISHING

Marriage: To Have and To Hold
Copyright © 2014 Hope For The Heart
All rights reserved.
Aspire Press, a division of Rose Publishing, Inc.
4733 Torrance Blvd., #259
Torrance, California 90503 USA
www.aspirepress.com

Register your book at www.aspirepress.com/register
Get inspiration via email, sign up at www.aspirepress.com

Printed in the United States of America
010114DP

CONTENTS

*D*ear Friend,

Having counseled thousands of married couples over the years, I am often asked, "What one thing do you believe sabotages more marriages than anything else?" Before I tell you my answer, I invite you to consider *yours*. What would you say? Unforgiveness? Lack of communication? Mishandling of finances? While these can certainly cause grief in a marriage, my answer may surprise you: *unrealistic expectations!*

Ruth Bell Graham—late wife of the noted evangelist—amplifies the point: "I pity the married couple who expects too much from one another. It is a foolish woman who expects her husband to be to her that which only Jesus Christ Himself can be: ready to forgive, totally understanding, unendingly patient, invariably tender and loving, unfailing in every area, anticipating every need, and making more than adequate provision. Such expectations put a man under an impossible strain. The same goes for the man who expects too much from his wife."[1]

My own mother knew a great deal about dashed expectations in marriage. My father, who was twice Mother's age when they wed, was also an adulterer. When asked about his frequent dalliances—which he made little effort to hide—dad would explain, "I'm not a Christian. I don't need to live by Christian ethics." Wounded to the core, Mother nevertheless tried valiantly to hide her tears. You see, to my father's way of thinking, tears were "a sign of mental illness." Mother had witnessed the plight of my father's firstborn son from a previous marriage. Pronounced mentally ill, dad had the boy permanently institutionalized. Would Mother be next?

I simply adored my mother. A kinder, more gracious and supportive woman I have never known. Over the years, witnessing her pain and senseless victimization filled me with bitter anger and resentment toward my father. Until, one day, unable to contain my hatred, it boiled over like a roaring volcano: "How can you be so nice to him?" I demanded of my mother, spitting the words between clinched teeth. What mom said next is one of the most memorable lessons I've ever learned about marriage. "Oh honey, he doesn't know the Lord," she said. "If he knew the Lord, he wouldn't act that way."

At the time, the words served only to infuriate me all the more. But over the years, as my walk with Christ deepened, I began to see their profound wisdom. And not just for marriage, but for every key relationship in life. As I matured, the Lord allowed me to grasp it: My godly mother was explaining that God was calling her to look beyond the *faults* of her flawed husband ... to see his *need*.

What would happen if every husband and wife did the same? Instead of focusing on the fault—the injustice, the "you had no right to treat me this way"—what if you looked below the surface? What if you asked, "What are the deepest root issues that are motivating my spouse to treat me this way?" "Is there anything I can do, Lord, to minister to those needs?"

What if the Prayer of St. Francis became the prayer of every husband and wife?

Lord, make me an instrument of your peace,
Where there is hatred, let me sow love;
Where there is injury, pardon;
Where there is doubt, faith;
Where there is despair, hope;
Where there is darkness, light;
Where there is sadness, joy.
O Divine Master,
Grant that I may not so much seek to be consoled,
as to console;
To be understood, as to understand;
To be loved, as to love.
For it is in giving that we receive.
It is in pardoning that we are pardoned,
And it is in dying that we are born to Eternal Life.
Amen.

The Bible teaches that God created marriage to make husbands and wives *holy*, not just to make them *happy*.[2] May this book help you discover wedded holiness—and happiness—that will keep your marriage flourishing "for as long as you both shall live."

Yours in the Lord's hope,

June Hunt

MARRIAGE
To Have and To Hold

"In the beginning God created the heavens and earth," a paradise of breathless beauty spawned in His own heart and populated with all the animals, *"each according to its kind"* (Genesis 1:1, 24). God was pleased with His perfect creation and yet He desired something else ... something different ... something like no other to populate His new world.

Many people forget—or don't even know—that our God is also the magnificent Creator of marriage. Unlike the creation of the animals, after forming the first man, the Lord fashions the first woman from the rib of the man! And then they become *one,* a living picture of God's desire for the union of man and woman in marriage.

Thus, after the creation of Adam and Eve, the first mention of the husband and wife relationship bursts forth on the scene:

> "... a man leaves his father and mother
> and is united to his wife,
> and they become one flesh."
> (Genesis 2:24)

DEFINITIONS

He may be a foremost voice on marriage and the family, but he's also the first to admit—there have been more than a few "flub-ups" along the way.

Jim Dobson is founder of both *Focus on the Family* and *Family Talk*, two nonprofit organizations committed to strengthening families through radio broadcasts, books, and conferences. He has been recognized by the United States Congress as a valued expert, having served on multiple government panels.

When it comes to marriage, Dr. Dobson says, "romantic love is the fuel that powers the female engine."[3] And, oh, does he learn this the hard way in his own life. On the day of his first major marital flub-up, he comes up short—he forgets it, he blows it, he ruins it!

> "If I am guilty—woe to me!"
> (Job 10:15)

WHAT IS God's Meaning of Marriage?

From the beginning, Jim and Shirley Dobson build their marriage on the solid foundation of biblical principles, including love and integrity—and their first Valentine's Day is sure to be unforgettable.

The atmosphere Shirley creates can't be more romantic: red candles glowing atop the table where a heart-shaped cake—a delicious pink cake to be admired, then devoured—welcomes home her sweetheart. A small gift awaits Jim, along with a love note befitting the amorous day. His bride eagerly anticipates his arrival at any moment as she meticulously prepares a special meal of her very best dishes.

In their first year of marriage, what could be more romantic than she being his Valentine and he being hers? On this romantic evening, there's just one glitch—Jim hasn't planned anything special because he doesn't even realize it is Valentine's Day![4] Unfortunately, rather than receiving the expression of love her heart hopes for, Shirley feels the pain firsthand of this verse:

> "Hope deferred makes the heart sick."
> (Proverbs 13:12)

▶ **Marriage** covenant is a binding agreement between a man and a woman who are legally and spiritually joined together as husband and wife.

Jesus says of the husband/wife relationship, *"So they are no longer two, but one flesh. Therefore what God has joined together, let no one separate"* (Matthew 19:6).

▶ **Marriage** ceremony refers to the rite of joining a man and a woman in wedlock.[5]

What Jim has planned for the day is a date with books and journals at a nearby library, where he spends about 10 hours on February 14—Valentine's Day.

Hungry and totally forgetting how special this day is, he grabs a hamburger at a restaurant and then decides to stop and visit his parents. Mom greets him with a big slice of apple pie, so now in Jim's mind there certainly isn't any reason to be in a hurry to go home. He later remembers—"that sealed my doom."[6]

Eventually he unlocks the front door around 10:00 p.m. and anything but romance fills the air. It's good that Jim and Shirley are totally committed to their marriage covenant, especially in the midst of unfulfilled expectations.

The concept of covenant is threaded throughout the Old and New Testaments, weaving a tapestry of steadfast love and loyalty between God and His people. The marriage vows mirror that same faithful devotion, expressing a lifetime commitment between two people and God.

The Bible says ...

> "But the steadfast love of the LORD
> is from everlasting to everlasting
> on those who fear him ...
> to those who keep his covenant
> and remember to do his commandments."
> (Psalm 103:17–18 ESV)

The Covenant Commitment

In biblical times, a covenant vow was binding and unbreakable. God made the marriage commitment to be a sacred covenant, a lifetime promise, a permanent pledge—"till death do we part."

1. **The marriage covenant** is not just between two people, but between two people *and* God.

   ▪ Covenants in the Old Testament were mutually binding agreements confirmed by an oath in God's name. The Hebrew word *beriyth*, used over 280 times in the Old Testament, is most often translated "covenant," which means "a binding agreement."[7]

   "On that day the Lord made a covenant with Abram and said, 'To your descendants I give this land ...'" (Genesis 15:18).

   ▪ If you are a covenant maker, your covenant is also with the Lord. Christian marriage ceremonies traditionally include the words of Jesus: *"... what God has joined together, let no one separate"* (Mark 10:9).

2. **The marriage covenant** requires self-sacrifice and a commitment till death.

   ▪ God initiated covenants with people and refused to forsake them.

   " ... they rejected my laws ... Yet in spite of this ... I will not reject them or abhor them so as to destroy them completely, breaking my covenant with them" (Leviticus 26:43–44).

- If you are a covenant keeper, you will refuse to forsake your marriage covenant.

  "May your fountain be blessed, and may you rejoice in the wife of your youth" (Proverbs 5:18).

3. **The marriage covenant** holds each person singly responsible to demonstrate a covenant of love and loyalty, even if the mate does not respond accordingly.

- Covenants require covenant makers to "die to self" through a willingness to make difficult personal sacrifices.

  "As far as it depends on you, live at peace with everyone" (Romans 12:18).

- Covenants can be based on the desires of one person or of many people.

  "... the LORD is the witness between you and the wife of your youth. You have been unfaithful to her, though she is your partner, the wife of your marriage covenant" (Malachi 2:14).

4. **The marriage covenant** keepers realize that keeping a lifetime commitment is a continual process of submitting their will to God, allowing Him to develop the character of Christ in them.

- As a covenant keeper, you are empowered by Christ (indwelling each believer) to remain faithful to your commitments.

  "I consider my life worth nothing to me; my only aim is to finish the race and complete the task the

Lord Jesus has given me—the task of testifying to the good news of God's grace" (Acts 20:24).

- Only the Lord promises us His power to be covenant keepers.

"His divine power has given us everything we need for a godly life through our knowledge of him who called us by his own glory and goodness. Through these he has given us his very great and precious promises, so that through them you may participate in the divine nature, having escaped the corruption in the world caused by evil desires" (2 Peter 1:3–4).

WHAT IS God's Order for Marriage?

Jim and Shirley's marriage is normally a model of God's four-point plan for the marital relationship, but the Valentine's Day fiasco does put the couple to the test.

Jim arrives home to a dark and deathly quiet apartment. Half-burned candles display dried up drips, and stale food lays heaped on pretty dishes. Jim's thoughts begin to race ... what have I forgotten? And then suddenly he sees red and white decorations on the table. He exclaims something that countless men (and women) who have forgotten Valentine's Day blurt out—"Oh no!"[8]

Here he just spent Valentine's evening with his mom—eating pie! Of course it's an accident, yet Jim will now be eating humble pie.

"Do nothing out of selfish ambition or vain conceit. Rather, in humility value others above yourselves, not looking to your own interests but each of you to the interests of the others." (Philippians 2:3–4)

God's Four-Point Plan for Marriage[9]

GENESIS 2:24–25

▶ **Separation**

"A man leaves his father and mother ..." (v. 24).

Both the husband and wife leave the authority of their parents and become a separate family unit. In marriage, the loyalty to a parent should never be stronger than the loyalty to a spouse.

▶ **Bonding**

"... and is united to his wife ..." (v. 24).

By an act of the will, bonding is a mental commitment to have a faithful, permanent relationship with a spouse regardless of whatever difficulties may arise.

▶ **Oneness**

"... they become one flesh" (v. 24).

Physical oneness is the consummation of sexual closeness. However, to achieve a lasting physical, emotional, and spiritual oneness, both spouses should look for ways to please, build up, and encourage the other. This can be accomplished by openly asking what is pleasurable and meaningful and by taking the time to enjoy one another.

▶ Intimacy

"... they felt no shame" (v. 25).

Emotional intimacy is encouraged when a married couple seek to be vulnerable and transparent. They honestly share with one another their feelings of frustration and failure, happiness and hopefulness, as well as their deepest disappointments and desires.

Spiritual intimacy is achieved when spouses continue to reveal to one another their innermost needs, confess their struggles to one another, pray for each other, and share what God is personally doing in their individual lives.

Rejected by In-Laws

QUESTION: **"My parents have rejected my wife ever since we've been married. They don't include her in family functions. I go without her to weddings, birthdays, and graduations. How can I get my parents to accept her?"**

ANSWER: As her husband, you are called to love your wife sacrificially as Christ loved the church (Ephesians 5:25). A tangible way to express your love for her is through actions that convey that you value and cherish her and are willing to "lay your life down" for her. Until now, you have been accepting of your parents' hurtful choice to exclude your wife from family functions.

For your parents to accept your wife, they need a motivating "reason" to accept her. Presently they have no motivation because no consequences have been attached to their failure to accept her. As long as you go alone to family affairs, you are communicating that excluding her is permissible. This is dishonoring to your wife. As a member of the extended family, it is only right that she be invited to normal family functions.

Therefore you must explain to your parents that in the future, either you and your wife will both come or you will both stay home. And you must be consistent 100% of the time unless you or your wife literally "can't make it."

Consider conveying to your parents the concepts contained in the following statements:

▶ "I love my family very much and always want to be at family occasions."

▶ "Because we are married, my wife is part of our family and should be included in our family functions."

▶ "Since the two of us are united as one, if you don't accept my wife, then you don't accept me."

▶ "When you don't respect her by ignoring her, you are also showing disrespect to me because she is my choice for a lifelong mate."

▶ "Beginning today, I expect my wife to be included in our family get-togethers and to be treated with acceptance or we will both stay home. Ultimately, the choice is yours."

> "A man will leave his father
> and mother and be united to his wife,
> and the two will become one flesh."
> (Ephesians 5:31)

WHAT IS God's Purpose for Marriage?

God's purpose for marriage is to model Christ and His relationship with the church, to be a beautiful portrait of sacrificial love. In this case, Shirley has sacrificed for Jim, and his heart is truly filled with remorse over forgetting the most romantic day of the year.

Jim and Shirley share a few words. Then Shirley sheds a few tears, heads straight to bed, and pulls the covers up to her ears. But her feelings of rejection are only temporary. Later, the pair discuss Jim's forgetfulness, and forgiveness from Shirley abounds.

Jim makes a firm commitment right then and there: "I learned a big lesson about Valentine's Day and determined never to forget it."[10]

This couple has been able to weather every storm they have encountered because they understand God's purpose for marriage. In the Bible, the marital relationship is designed to represent Christ's committed relationship with His "bride," meaning the church, which is comprised of all *true* Christians. In the same way that Christ sacrificially gave Himself to the church, you and your mate should willingly sacrifice your individual desires for the sake of your marriage covenant.

> "Husbands, love your wives, just as
> Christ loved the church and
> gave himself up for her."
> (Ephesians 5:25)

▶ Partnership

- God has given you and your mate to one another as partners for life. True companionship grows within the marriage relationship when there is emotional, spiritual, and physical unity.

  "My beloved is mine and I am his ... "
  (Songs of Songs 2:16).

▶ Parenting

- God's first command in Scripture was for Adam and Eve to be *"fruitful"* and *"multiply"* (Genesis 9:7). God desires that the earth be filled with godly offspring.

  "Marry and have sons and daughters; find wives for your sons and give your daughters in marriage, so that they too may have sons and daughters. Increase in number there; do not decrease" (Jeremiah 29:6).

▶ Pleasure

- The marriage relationship and your mate are God's special gifts to you. True enjoyment of your mate will grow out of self-control and a servant's heart.

  "I belong to my beloved, and his desire is for me" (Song of Songs 7:10).

  In the intimate relationship of marriage, spouses become well aware of one another's shortcomings! God uses the weaknesses and strengths of both spouses to sharpen and conform each of them into the image of Christ.

  "As iron sharpens iron, so one person sharpens another" (Proverbs 27:17).

Jim and Shirley Dobson have been married for more than 50 years, enjoying a monogamous relationship that pleases God and displays His perfect design.

Stemming from the Valentine's Day disaster, Jim has learned the importance of enjoying romantic activities with Shirley, like going on dates and visiting places of sentimental importance. Jim frequently reminds men that marriages need to be nurtured "or they can wither like a plant without water."[11]

The following Scripture can be applied to nurturing in a marital context.

> "And let us consider how we may
> spur one another on toward
> love and good deeds."
> (Hebrews 10:24)

From the beginning, God had a very specific design for marriage, and He has not wavered from it. Individuals and cultures have altered it to suit their own purposes, but God's design for marriage consists of one man and one woman—committed to one another for life.

▶ **Monogamy** means being married to only one person or to only one person at a time.[12] Monogamy stands in contrast to polygamy.

Jesus said, *"At the beginning the Creator 'made them male and female,' and said, 'For this reason a man will leave his father and mother and be united* to his wife, and the two will become one flesh.' So they are no longer two, but one flesh. Therefore what God has joined together, let no one separate" (Matthew 19:4–6).

▶ **Polygamy** means being married to two or more people at the same time.[13]

ARGUMENT: "God approved of polygamy in the Old Testament and changed His mind in the New Testament."

ANSWER: God has never changed. From the beginning His original design for the covenant marriage was monogamy. Polygamy was never mandated or ever endorsed by God. The first mention of the marriage union makes this point clear.

"The LORD God said, 'It is not good for the man to be alone. I will make a helper [not helpers] *suitable for him.' ... That is why a man leaves his father and mother and is united to his wife* [not wives] *..."* (Genesis 2:18, 24).

▶ **Remarriage** means a second or repeated marriage.

ARGUMENT: "Although my husband died several years ago, to honor his memory, I must not consider remarriage"

ANSWER: No, God's Word says you are free to marry again as long as the person is a believer.

"A woman is bound to her husband as long as he lives. But if her husband dies, she is free to marry anyone she wishes, but he must belong to the Lord" (1 Corinthians 7:39).

We serve a God who is intensely interested in our lives on earth. The plans He has set out for us are for our benefit—both on earth and for eternity. His guidelines are to allow us the best in both worlds. He jealously guards His children because His heart is for our greatest good, and He ordained that the choices we make will determine benefits for not only this life, but for eternity as well.

> **"Whatever you do, work at it**
> **with all your heart, as working for the Lord,**
> **not for human masters,**
> **since you know that you will receive**
> **an inheritance from the Lord as a reward.**
> **It is the Lord Christ you are serving."**
> **(Colossians 3:23–24)**

Throughout Scripture, God has given us insight into His heart regarding marriage. Clearly, His mind-set has always been that the marriage relationship is ...

▶ To be honored and kept pure

"Marriage should be honored by all, and the marriage bed kept pure, for God will judge the adulterer and all the sexually immoral" (Hebrews 13:4).

▶ To provide companionship and intimacy

"However, each one of you also must love his wife as he loves himself, and the wife must respect her husband" (Ephesians 5:33).

▶ To exhibit unity

"Jesus knew their thoughts and said to them, 'Every kingdom divided against itself will be ruined, and every city or household divided against itself will not stand'" (Matthew 12:25).

▶ To last a lifetime

"For example, by law a married woman is bound to her husband as long as he is alive, but if her husband dies, she is released from the law that binds her to him" (Romans 7:2).

▶ To not end in divorce

"'I hate divorce!' says the LORD, the God of Israel" (Malachi 2:16 NLT).

▶ To avoid contamination by hardened hearts

"Jesus replied, 'Moses permitted you to divorce your wives because your hearts were hard. But it was not this way from the beginning. I tell you that anyone who divorces his wife, except for sexual immorality, and marries another woman commits adultery'" (Matthew 19:8–9).

▶ To share oneness of spirit, soul, and body

"Do not be yoked together with unbelievers. For what do righteousness and wickedness have in common? Or what fellowship can light have with darkness?" (2 Corinthians 6:14).

Biblical Submission

QUESTION: "Because the Bible says in Ephesians 5:23, *'The husband is the head of the wife,'* must a wife submit to being abused by her husband?"

ANSWER: Submission is a voluntary yielding to the power, authority, or desire of another, especially in a marriage relationship in deference and obedience to God. Although the wife is to submit to the "headship" (leadership) of her husband, the Bible never implies that she is to submit to any abuse from her husband. She is to respect his *position*, not be victimized by his *power*.

▶ If a husband is physically abusing his wife or engaging her in any illegal activity and "reminding" her of the submission Scripture, her response should be biblical—by calling for help (even the police)—submitting to the governing authorities (Romans 13:1).

▶ If he gets angry and shouts, "You aren't being Christian," her response should be biblical—by getting out of harm's way. Proverbs 22:24 says, *"Do not make friends with a hot-tempered person, do not associate with one easily angered."*

▶ If he tries to manipulate her into not taking legal action against him, her response should be biblical—by allowing him to suffer the consequences of his actions. Proverbs 19:19 says, *"A hot-tempered person must pay the penalty; rescue them, and you will have to do it again."*

Remember, physical abuse is *illegal*. Help can be sought through the civil authorities. It is important to keep in mind that God hates violence! He encourages us to be wise and to seek shelter from personal danger. *"The prudent see danger and take refuge, but the simple keep going and pay the penalty"* (Proverbs 27:12).

[Contact HOPE FOR THE HEART at 1-800-488-HOPE (4673) for specific steps in dealing with wife abuse.]

Conversely, biblical submission is *mutual* for both the wife *and* the husband. While wives are explicitly exhorted to submit to their husbands, husbands are called to radically love their wives by following Jesus' example of self-sacrifice.

▶ If men are called to love in this way, the concept of submission to Christ is certainly present.

▶ At the minimum, a husband is called to submit his own self-interest to the interest of his wife in following the example of Christ.

When the term "submission" is used to manipulate a wife in order to perpetuate abuse or when submission is one-sided on the part of the wife with no similar surrender to Christ on the part of the husband, those types of submission are unbiblical.

God's Word says ...

> **"Wives, submit yourselves to your own husbands as you do to the Lord. ... Husbands, love your wives, just as Christ loved the church and gave himself up for her." (Ephesians 5:22, 25)**

CHARACTERISTICS

He refers to it as "Vive la Difference!"[14]

Dr. James Dobson heartily endorses the French mind-set: *Long live the differences between the sexes!* This expert in child psychology says those differences created and ordained by God should be celebrated. That is all except one, the major difference he and his wife have struggled with since their honeymoon: *preferred room temperature.* The "temperature war" is a common battlefield for both husbands and wives, because typically women have a slower metabolism than men.

"I am very hot-blooded," Jim explains, "and prefer a Siberian climate if given a choice. Shirley has ice in her veins and even shivers in the California sunshine. She has concluded that if we can have only one flesh between us, she's going to make it sweat! She will slip over to the thermostat at home and spin the dial to at least eighty-five degrees. All the bacteria in the house jump for joy and begin reproducing like crazy. In a few minutes I am starting to glow and begin throwing open doors and windows to get relief."[15]

Even in spite of our physical differences, Scripture encourages us in our day-to-day living to give preference to one another—a practice the Dobsons have honed over a half century.

"Do nothing out of selfish ambition
or vain conceit. Rather, in humility value
others above yourselves,
not looking to your own interests but each
of you to the interests of the others."
(Philippians 2:3–4)

WHAT ARE Male versus Female Tendencies?

One of the major differences between males and females is their priorities for the home.

Women generally are more concerned about furnishings and décor, paying attention to the details of decorating. Jim recalls buying a gas barbecue unit that needed to be installed by a plumber. When the job in their backyard was finished, the unit stood about eight inches too high; immediately their priorities differed.

> **JIM:** "It's true, the plumber made a mistake. The barbecue unit is a bit too high. By the way, what's for dinner tonight?"

> **SHIRLEY:** "I don't think I can stand that thing sticking up in the air like that!"[16]

He could have gone the rest of his life without another thought about the height, but for Shirley—as primary caretaker of the home—this was big-time trouble! Recognizing the difference between males and females, Jim had the plumber return and reinstall the barbecue unit.

In truth, husbands need to address even the minor concerns of their wives, and wives in turn should be in tune to their husband's concerns. Thoughtfully serving one another reflects the heart of Christ, as seen through His words:

> "For even the Son of Man did not come to be served, but to serve, and to give his life as a ransom for many."
> (Mark 10:45)

What do you know about the man or woman in your life? Are you perplexed or even angered by your loved one's behavior and responses? When Scripture says, "... God 'made them male and female,'" it simply means that God made them different, and this dissimilarity goes deeper than the obvious physical differences.

God constructed them with internal distinctiveness. Males and females simply think and experience life differently. Understanding masculinity and femininity is a clue to understanding and loving your mate.

The Bible says ...

> "At the beginning of creation God 'made them male and female.'"
> (Mark 10:6)

Males Tend to Be More ...	Females Tend to Be More ...
Visual	Auditory
Objective	Subjective
Goal-oriented	Relationship-oriented
Emotionally closed	Emotionally open
Single-focused	Multi-focused
Focused on the bottom line	Attentive to details
Quantity-oriented	Quality-oriented
Stimulated by sight	Stimulated by touch
Concentrated on sex	Content with being held
Power-oriented	People-oriented
In need of significance	In need of security

These tendencies are not weighed on a scale of "right or wrong." They are complimentary and God-given to bring balance and depth to a relationship. As you review the two lists, you could conclude that within your relationship certain role reversals exist. Don't think something is wrong with either of you. Instead, note the differences and recognize that God is the God of unique individuals and has put the two of you together for His divine purpose.

The Bible says ...

> "God saw all that he had made,
> and it was very good."
> (Genesis 1:31)

Have you ever wondered why God made males and females so completely different, yet He still expects married couples to bond within a lifelong relationship? God has an exceptional answer.

He wants to mold the character of His children into the likeness of Christ. In a marriage relationship, He uses the distinct qualities, strengths, and desires of women and men to help shape their character to reflect Christ, while preserving their unique traits and personalities.

> "And we all, who with unveiled faces
> contemplate the Lord's glory,
> are being transformed into his image with
> ever-increasing glory, which comes from
> the Lord, who is the Spirit."
> (2 Corinthians 3:18)

Practical Desires of a Wife

Discuss with each other the following two lists of the "Desires of the Heart" to see if they describe both of you. Point out any differences to help your partner get the best picture of who you really are. Don't box one another into that picture. Be open to growing and encouraging one another to be who God wants you to be as your wounds heal and you open up to new experiences. Embrace each other's unique desires.

HER HEART'S DESIRES REGARDING COMMUNICATION:

▶ "**Be interested** in my life, **encourage** me."

▶ "**Listen** to my problems, big and small."

▶ "**Talk** about my work."

▶ "**Connect** with my family/our children."

▶ "**Share** with me your dreams, plans, and goals."

▶ "**Give** me compliments."

▶ "**Ask** about my feelings."

▶ "**Reveal** to me your true feelings."

HER HEART'S DESIRES REGARDING APPRECIATION:

▶ "**Let me know** you want me."

▶ "**Show** interest in my life."

▶ "**Show** others you love me."

▶ "**Take** me out alone—without other family or friends."

▶ "**Include** me with your friends."

▶ "**Express** gratitude for what I'm contributing to our marriage."

▶ "**Help** out with the family chores and disciplining the children—without being asked."

▶ "**Be consistent** with your expressions of appreciation."

Her Heart's Desires regarding Being Understood:

▶ "**Learn** my likes and dislikes."

▶ "**Comfort** me when I'm sad."

▶ "**Calm** me when I'm upset."

▶ "**Care** for me when I'm sick."

▶ "**Show** enthusiasm over my accomplishments."

▶ "**Reassure** me when my efforts fail."

▶ "**Be** affectionate toward me—outside the bedroom."

▶ "**Let** me hear that you'll love me forever."

> "When anxiety was great within me,
> your consolation brought me joy."
> (Psalm 94:19)

Practical Desires of a Husband

His Heart's Desires regarding Communication:

▶ "**Ask** for my opinions."

▶ "**Compliment** my accomplishments."

▶ "**Comment** on my work."

▶ "**Give** me *constructive* criticism in a loving way."

▶ "**Trust me** to say the right things to people or to ask for your help if I need it."

▶ "**Don't drop hints**, but rather **speak plainly** about your expectations for household projects and tasks."

▶ "**Recognize** my need for periodic intervals of quiet time to think, unwind, or just relax."

▶ "**Praise** my leadership when it's deserved."

HIS HEART'S DESIRES REGARDING APPRECIATION:

▶ "**Help** me feel that you want me."

▶ "**Show respect** toward me at home and in public."

▶ "**Engage** my mind."

▶ "**Express** gratitude toward me."

▶ "**Be there** for me."

▶ "**Demonstrate** loyalty to me."

▶ "**Be my companion**, not my competitor or critic."

▶ "**Value** me for the contributions I make to our home."

HIS HEART'S DESIRES REGARDING BEING UNDERSTOOD:

▶ "**Learn** who I really am."

▶ "**Listen** to me."

▶ "**Be** there for me."

▶ "**Realize** that I will sometimes come home tired and frustrated."

▶ "**Comfort** me when I fail."

▶ "**Care** for me when I'm sick."

▶ "**Be** physically and sexually responsive to me."

▶ "**Allow** me to lead our family."

> "Place me like a seal over your heart,
> like a seal on your arm;
> for love is as strong as death,
> its jealousy unyielding as the grave.
> It burns like blazing fire, like a mighty flame.
> Many waters cannot quench love;
> rivers cannot sweep it away."
> (Song of Songs 8:6–7)

WHAT IS Biblical Authority/ Submission?

Jesus, who was given *"all authority in heaven and on earth"* (Matthew 28:18), is our example. His life demonstrates submission to the Father, to His earthly parents, and to the governing authorities. Jesus' life reflects a heart of humility, and husbands and wives are to reflect His heart to one another and to those around them.

"Who [Jesus], being in very nature God, did not consider equality with God something to be used to his own advantage; rather, he made himself nothing by taking the very nature of a servant, being made in human likeness. And being found in appearance as a man, he humbled himself by becoming obedient to death—even death on a cross!" (Philippians 2:6–8).

▶ **The prideful heart** rebels against authority.

▶ **The humbled heart** is biblically submissive.

> "Pride brings a person low,
> but the lowly in spirit gain honor."
> (Proverbs 29:23)

PRIDEFUL HEART	HUMBLED HEART
Haughty	Humble
Selfish	Unselfish
Impatient	Patient
Controlling	Self-controlled
Immature	Mature
Manipulative	Meek
Critical	Compassionate
Quarrelsome	Quiet in spirit
Ill-tempered	Even-tempered
Independent	Dependent on the Lord

God-Given Authority Structures

A relationship of submission exists not only between husbands and wives, but also in other relationships—and even within the Godhead. The Lord God instituted and exemplifies this balance of power and authority.

> "Whoever rebels against the authority is rebelling against what God has instituted, and those who do so will bring judgment on themselves." (Romans 13:2)

▶ **God the Father** submits judgment to the Son.

The Holy Trinity (of Father, Son, and Holy Spirit) exists in mutual interdependence where at different times each is submissive to or defers to the other. Each works for the glory and benefit of the other and provides the ultimate example of self-giving love.

"The Father judges no one, but has entrusted all judgment to the Son, that all may honor the Son just as they honor the Father" (John 5:22–23).

▶ **God the Son** (Jesus) submits to the Father.

Each Person of the Trinity is equal—the Father, Son, and Holy Spirit are equally God. Jesus, the eternal Son of God, submitted to the will of the heavenly Father. The heavenly Father planned for our redemption, and the Son paid the price for our redemption. Jesus Christ, the Son of God, was submissive to His heavenly Father's will.

"... I do nothing on my own but speak just what the Father has taught me" (John 8:28).

▶ **God the Holy Spirit** submits to the Father and the Son.

Jesus announced to His disciples that when He left this earth, He would not leave them comfortless, but that He would send them another Comforter, another Counselor, whom He called the Spirit of Truth. The Holy Spirit was sent by the Father, speaks only what He hears, and guides each authentic Christian.

"When he, the Spirit of truth, comes, he will guide you into all truth. He will not speak on his own; he will speak only what he hears, and he will tell you what is yet to come" (John 16:13).

▶ **Men** are to submit to the headship of Christ.

"I want you to realize that the head of every man is Christ ..." (1 Corinthians 11:3).

▶ **Wives** are to be submissive to their husbands.

"Wives, in the same way submit yourselves to your own husbands ..." (1 Peter 3:1).

▶ **Husbands** are to submit their actions to love for their wife.

"Husbands, love your wives, just as Christ loved the church and gave himself up for her" (Ephesians 5:25).

▶ **Children** must obey their parents.

"Children, obey your parents in everything, for this pleases the Lord" (Colossians 3:20).

▶ **Everyone** (single and married adults, widows and widowers, and the divorced) are to submit directly to God while being responsive to the counsel of their parents, godly advisors, and other authority figures.

"Listen to your father, who gave you life, and do not despise your mother when she is old" (Proverbs 23:22).

"We must obey God rather than human beings!" (Acts 5:29).

▶ **Employees** are to submit to their employers.

"Obey your earthly masters in everything; and do it, not only when their eye is on you and to curry their favor, but with sincerity of heart and reverence for the Lord. Whatever you do, work at it with all your heart, as working for the Lord, not for human masters" (Colossians 3:22–23).

▶ **Everyone** is to submit to the governing authorities.

"Submit yourselves for the Lord's sake to every human authority ..." (1 Peter 2:13).

▶ **Everyone** is to submit to one another.

"Submit to one another out of reverence for Christ" (Ephesians 5:21).

Obedience and Submission

QUESTION: "What is the difference between obedience and submission?"

ANSWER: Both obedience and submission are clear directives from God. However, consider the difference between conformity to the letter of the law and yielding to the spirit of the law. Mere outward compliance does not reflect God's heart. God's desire is that submission to His ordained authorities be done with inner attitudes of respect, loyalty, gentleness, and ultimate trust in Him for the outcome.

▶ **Submission** is to *voluntarily yield* to the will of another.

- **Obedience** is to *comply* with the commands of another.

▶ **Submission** is an *inner attitude* of the heart.

- **Obedience** is an *outer act* of conformity.

"The LORD does not look at the things people look at. People look at the outward appearance, but the LORD looks at the heart." (1 Samuel 16:7)

CAUSES

Dr. Dobson often says he has a wonderful marriage, but he never says he has a *perfect* marriage. In every marriage "there will be times of conflict and disagreement. There will be periods of emotional blandness when you can generate nothing but a yawn for one another."[17]

This time of emotional flatness is when the word *commitment* means the most in marriage—sticking it out instead of giving up. Christian couples should always remember that they have an enemy who is eager to destroy their sacred union. Yet Jim Dobson is adamant: "Nothing short of death"[18] should come between any couple.

Far too many people enter marriage expecting a personal "payoff." *She's going to make me feel significant—forever. He's going to make me happy— forever.* Eventually, these unrealistic expectations can become lost hopes and dreams that ultimately produce a root of bitterness. Then all too soon, that bitter root produces bitter fruit. The result of bitterness is found in Scripture:

"See to it that no one falls short of the grace of God and that no bitter root grows up to cause trouble and defile many."
(Hebrews 12:15)

When unrealistic expectations reside in marriage and those expectations aren't met, couples can turn to certain counterfeits for a false sense of comfort. How easy to get caught in the trap of focusing on "whatever meets *my* needs." That can lead to *expecting* others to "do what *I* want them to do."

And who better to do that than the mate who at one time caught our eye?

We think we've entered the storybook tale of "happily ever after." But then reality hits! We keep expecting from our spouse what we can't get. We think our empty bucket will now be filled, and stay forever full. "This is what I expect you to do for *me*."

But our bucket has holes in it—holes that no person can fill. Our unrealistic expectations are founded on faulty assumptions—not words of wisdom. We are deceived and don't even know it.

How interesting that the biblical book of wisdom contrasts deception and wisdom:

> "The wisdom of the prudent is
> to give thought to their ways,
> but the folly of fools is deception."
> (Proverbs 14:8)

▶ Common Unrealistic Assumptions

- "Marriage will provide me with love and acceptance."
- "Marriage will guarantee me affection and sexual intimacy."
- "Marriage will rescue me from my present circumstances."
- "Marriage will furnish me with financial security."
- "Marriage will afford me significance and social acceptance."
- "Marriage will grant me broader career opportunities."
- "Marriage will protect me from loneliness."
- "Marriage will surround me with a loving, supportive family."
- "Marriage will assure me that someone will take care of me."
- "Marriage will allow me to change my mate."

▶ Common Faulty Conclusions

- "I must be unlovable. You don't love or accept me."
- "I realize I'm not worth the attention. You no longer spend time with me."
- "I now see that we should have never married. This is not a marriage made in heaven."
- "I know we'll never be happy. I may as well end it all now."
- "I've tried everything and nothing works. I feel completely hopeless."

- "I thought we'd go out every weekend for fun, but now we never go out."
- "I thought a family would give me purpose, but no one even cares."
- "I wanted someone to share my heart with, but now it's just sports, TV, and sleep."
- "Life's too short to keep living like this. I think we'll both be happier living separate lives."
- "I only hear 'You'll never change.' I just can't take it anymore."

Instead of living with unrealistic expectations regarding what you don't have, be grateful to God for what you *do* have.

The Bible says ...

"Godliness with contentment is great gain."
(1 Timothy 6:6)

The Impact of Infirmity within Marriage

QUESTION: "My husband has become permanently disabled, and now our sexual relationship is nonexistent. How can we reclaim the closeness we used to share through physical intimacy when sex is no longer an option?"

ANSWER: Marriage relationships undergo many changes when a mate becomes severely ill or incapacitated. Depending on the level of disability and dependence, roles within the relationship can be altered. A deeper dependency will also impact the dynamics of a marriage. With everyday activities affected, sexual intimacy can become difficult or disappear altogether. Since intimacy is not just limited to the sexual act, closeness can be maintained emotionally, spiritually, and by physical affection.

▶ **Emotional intimacy:**

- *Communicate* openly and honestly in expressing your grief over what you have both lost.
- *Share* treasured memories and experiences that reinforce your love for each other.
- *Be* grateful for what you have as a couple, rather than focusing on what you no longer have.

▶ **Spiritual intimacy:**

- *Read* and study the Bible together to grow spiritually closer to God and each other.
- *Pray* with each other and for each other, relying on the Lord for His strength, hope, and peace.
- *Thank* God that, as believers in Christ, one day you will both be spiritually and physically whole in heaven.

▶ **Physical intimacy:**

- *Continue* to share a bed unless medical necessity dictates separate sleeping arrangements.
- *Share* nonsexual physical touch that you have both found pleasurable—holding hands, hugging, giving back or foot rubs, stroking hair, snuggling together, holding each other close.
- *Maintain* closeness through activities or events you both enjoy as participants or spectators.

Many couples exchange wedding vows that include the promises, "In sickness and in health, till death do us part." But the reality is often not truly tested until serious illness or debilitation strikes. Then those impactful words—the wedding vows—become vividly real as loving, sacrificial service toward the afflicted mate is fully demonstrated. Jesus Himself speaks of the caring, compassionate person.

> "I was hungry and you gave me
> something to eat, I was thirsty and you gave
> me something to drink ...
> I needed clothes and you clothed me,
> I was sick and you looked after me ... "
> (Matthew 25:35–36)

WHAT IS the Makeup of Five Troubled Marriages?

It could have been a money-troubled marriage—not between Jim and Shirley Dobson, but between his father and mother.

Now with the Lord, Jim's dad was a traveling evangelist who received a pittance for his revival efforts. But even then, he always seemed to turn it into a blessing. The younger Dobson remembers a time when his dad returned home after preaching for ten days at a tiny church and his mother inquired: "How much did they pay you?"[19] He stammered as his eyes dropped to the floor, and then a smile crossed his face.

Those were signs his mother recognized because she replied: "Oh, I get it. You gave the money away again, didn't you?"[20] The generosity of the elder Dobson was not missed by God, who frequently compensated his kindness with unexpected checks in the Dobson mailbox. He was a great example of how to have a giving heart and how to trust God to meet your financial needs.

> "Each of you should give what you have
> decided in your heart to give,
> not reluctantly or under compulsion,
> for God loves a cheerful giver."
> (2 Corinthians 9:7)

God will use the marital relationship as a chisel to chip away character flaws. When your marriage consists of the following characteristics, that's a red flag indicating the need for one or both of you to change. God's intent is for both partners to move from selfishness to sacrificial behavior that reflects the sacrificial love of Christ.

1. **The Make-Believe Marriage**—lacking honest and intimate communication by ...

▶ **Not working** through problems: stubbornness

▶ **Not accepting** responsibility: defensiveness

▶ **Not acknowledging** your mate's feelings: rejection

▶ **Not being** concerned about your mate's needs: selfishness

▶ **Not displaying** affection: apathy

▶ **Not confronting**: insecurity

▶ **Not being** direct: manipulation

The make-believe marriage is a marriage in name only. Two people are going through the outward rituals of a marriage, yet one or both seem to be selfishly pursuing individual personal goals. The way to enjoy intimate communication is to be as concerned about your partner's needs as you are about your own. Pray for the Lord to pour His wisdom into your mind so that you can share from a pure heart.

The Bible says, *"The wise in heart are called discerning, and gracious words promote instruction"* (Proverbs 16:21).

2. **The Maladjusted Marriage**—experiencing sexual difficulty because of ...

▶ **Inhibition**: fearfulness (due to false guilt, sexual abuse, psychological problems)

▶ **Impatience:** insensitivity (demanding, coercive)

▶ **Infidelity**: self-centeredness (adultery, pornography)

▶ **Fatigue**: exhaustion (excessive busyness, overcommitment)

▶ **Anger**: bitterness (unforgiveness, manipulation)

The maladjusted marriage doesn't experience the emotional expression of physical "oneness." As an act of love, God's design is that both partners yield their bodies to one another. True sexual fulfillment comes through seeking to provide pleasure to the other in ways that do not violate the conscience of either.

The Bible says, *"The husband should fulfill his marital duty to his wife, and likewise the wife to her husband. The wife does not have authority over her own body but yields it to her husband. In the same way, the husband does not have authority over his own body but yields it to his wife"* (1 Corinthians 7:3–4).

3. **The Mixed-Up Marriage**—having conflicting values over ...

▶ **Religious beliefs**
- "We should attend church every Sunday."
- "Church attendance is not important."

▶ **Parenting responsibilities**
- "Children should be taught to obey."
- "Children should be given total freedom."

▶ **Marital commitments**
- "Adultery is unthinkable."
- "An affair could be healthy for a marriage."

▶ **Social convictions**
- "We will not have alcohol in our home."
- "There is nothing wrong with social drinking."

▶ **Friendship choices**
- "Your friends are a bad influence on us."
- "They have always been my friends, and always will be."

▶ **Moral principles**
- "Abortion is always wrong because it is murder."
- "Abortion is okay and should be the mother's choice."

The mixed-up marriage creates power struggles, tension, and criticism. When basic values are in conflict, the couple has great difficulty developing oneness in mind, will, and emotions. God's design for the married couple is that they be like-minded, having the same desires and purposes.

The Bible says, *"Make my joy complete by being like-minded, having the same love, being one in spirit and of one mind"* (Philippians 2:2).

4. The Money-Troubled Marriage—
experiencing financial disagreements over ...

▶ How will the family income be earned and spent?

▶ How will credit cards be used, or will they be used at all?

▶ How will credit card misuse be avoided and handled if it occurs?

▶ How will the financial budget be determined and followed?

▶ How will financial priorities be established?

▶ How will the lack of money for essentials be handled?

Conflicting answers to these questions and other financial difficulties can result in an unhealthy focus on money and material needs. God desires that a marriage be free of an emphasis on money by following biblical principles pertaining to money and trusting Him for financial security.

The Bible says, *"Keep your lives free from the love of money and be content with what you have, because God has said, 'Never will I leave you; never will I forsake you'"* (Hebrews 13:5).

5. **The Misaligned Marriage**—failing to recognize or respond to God-given roles ...

▶ **Failure of the husband ...**

- He is not a spiritual leader.
- He is not financially responsible.
- He defers decision making.
- He doesn't initiate problem solving.
- He neglects his wife emotionally.
- He consistently gives in to her demands.
- He doesn't communicate his desires and needs.

▶ **Failure of the wife ...**

- She doesn't have a gentle spirit.
- She tries to control her husband.
- She becomes involved in power struggles.
- She stubbornly holds to her opinions.
- She withdraws emotionally.
- She is bitter and sarcastic.
- She seeks revenge!

God's plan for the husband is to feel a sense of *significance* through both providing for his family and receiving the love and respect of his wife. Likewise, he is used by God to be a source of *security* for his wife through his love, acceptance, sensitivity to her desires, and his unselfish commitment to their marriage.[21] This is all in God's marvelous plan for fulfillment in marriage—His design preplanned for us.

"For we are God's handiwork, created in Christ Jesus to do good works, which God prepared in advance for us to do" (Ephesians 2:10).

Sexually Nonresponsive Mate

QUESTION: "I can't respond to my husband's sexual desires—but why?"

ANSWER: Negative or distorted parental views or comments regarding any topic related to sex can set up anxiety, apprehension, uncertainty, uneasiness, distrust, even fear in the hearts of young people. For example, if a father is concerned that his daughter could be taken advantage of sexually, he might say, "Sex is dirty." These words alone could block a healthy understanding of any physical closeness or tenderness. A child raised in an environment where caring, warmth, and endearment are absent will undoubtedly be apprehensive about displays of physical affection.

▶ **Unhealthy parental attitudes**
  - Lack of displayed affection within the family
  - Failure to communicate God's perspective on sex and marriage at the appropriate times

▶ **Childhood sexual abuse**
  - Flashbacks of sexual abuse as a child
  - Childhood experimentation with sexual activity

▶ **Remorse**
  - Guilt from having premarital sex
  - Guilt over having an abortion

▶ **Adultery**
  - Betrayal from misplaced affections
  - Shame, robbing a married couple of healthy sexual expression

▶ **Physical problems**
- Physical pain experienced while engaging in sexual activity
- Failure to consult a medical doctor (gynecologist or urologist)

▶ **Forced sex**
- Sexual intimacy triggers traumatic memories of rape.
- A spouse who demands unwanted sexual activity commits "mate rape." (Sexual expression should be a voluntary act of love.)

▶ **Pornography**
- Sexually explicit magazines, movies, books, and television.
- Unrealistic and extreme portrayals of sex may dull normal sexual response to a mate.

▶ **Fatigue**
- Many workaholics find themselves too exhausted to enjoy physical intimacy.
- The continual demands of childcare and housekeeping contribute to fatigue.

God designed sexual intimacy for marriage. To withhold sexual expression is not only rejection of your mate but also rejection of God's stated will.

"The husband should fulfill his marital duty to his wife, and likewise the wife to her husband. The wife does not have authority over her own body but yields it to her husband. In the same way, the husband does not have authority over his own body but yields it to his wife. Do not deprive each other except perhaps

by mutual consent and for a time, so that you may devote yourselves to prayer. Then come together again so that Satan will not tempt you because of your lack of self-control" (1 Corinthians 7:3–5).

WHAT ARE Misconceptions about Marriage Partners?

Certain wants and wishes, desires and expectations exist between wives and husbands both before and during their marriage relationship. One problem with these often unspoken "wants" is that many couples enter into marriage without ever discussing them with one another. They then end up being disappointed and feeling dejected when they aren't met. The end result is the eruption of fights and quarrels between them.

Just as Jesus encouraged us to speak freely with God, we should be able to communicate honestly and openly with our spouse.

> "Do not let any unwholesome talk
> come out of your mouths,
> but only what is helpful for building others
> up according to their needs,
> that it may benefit those who listen."
> (Ephesians 4:29)

Some examples of what each spouse might expect to "get" from the other include ...

▶ WIFE: "I'll get security."

   HUSBAND: "I'll get significance."

▶ WIFE: "I'll get to be the queen of the castle."
HUSBAND: "I'll get to be king of my castle."

▶ WIFE: "I'll get a home and get to manage it."
HUSBAND: "I'll get to manage my wife."

▶ WIFE: "I'll get a husband to take care of me."
HUSBAND: "I'll get a wife to take care of me."

▶ WIFE: "I'll get a husband who ...

- "Will repair anything broken"
- "Will always take out the trash"
- "Will spend quality time with the children"
- "Will romance me every week"
- "Will treat me like we are dating"

HUSBAND: "I'll get a wife who ...

- "Will always cook perfect meals"
- "Will always keep a spotless house"
- "Will make the children obey perfectly"
- "Will always want to please me"
- "Will treat me like we are dating"

▶ WIFE: "I'll get unconditional love from my husband."

HUSBAND: "I'll get unconditional love from my wife."

The Bible addresses a critical component to having valid expectations not only met, but exceeded.

"And they exceeded our expectations: They gave themselves first of all to the Lord, and then by the will of God also to us." (2 Corinthians 8:5)

Dr. Dobson readily admits he married his best friend and recognizes that his marriage is sacred before God.

The stabilizing factor in his long-lasting marriage is unequivocally *prayer*, seeking God's help and hand of blessing upon their entire family. When Jim and Shirley's daughter, Danae, begins driving at 16, the couple commits to pray for their children every night. One night they are particularly exhausted and collapse into bed, forgetting about their nightly prayer ritual. Both almost asleep, Shirley eventually remembers they have forgotten to pray and gently inquires: "Jim, we haven't prayed for our kids yet today. Don't you think we should talk to the Lord?"[22]

Despite the desire to remain in their warm bed, the couple obediently kneel before the Lord, interceding for their children. Meanwhile, Danae and her girlfriend pick up dinner at a fast-food restaurant then park up the road to eat. A policeman drives by shining his large spotlight in all directions, obviously searching for someone. Minutes later, the girls hear noises under their car and are stunned when a man crawls out, undoubtedly the policeman's target.

The suspect tries to force the car door open, but thankfully all doors are locked. At that very moment, Danae speeds off and the girls are safe. As it turns out, her parents are praying at that very moment![23] This frightening scenario both substantiates the need for and demonstrates the power of prayer. And that very same power can also lead to satisfying, long-lasting marriages. Scripture affirms ...

> **"The prayer of a righteous person is powerful and effective." (James 5:16)**

Major Priorities for Marriage

Have you and your mate established priorities for your marriage? Consider making these priorities *your priorities*:

▶ "My marriage is sacred before God."

▶ "My mate and I pray together daily."

▶ "My mate is my best friend."

▶ "My mate is someone I really like."

▶ "My mate and I have the same values and goals."

▶ "My mate is becoming more interesting as our marriage matures."

▶ "My mate and I deeply desire that our marriage succeed."

▶ "My marriage is a long-term, lifelong commitment."

When your thoughts are right, your priorities are right, which enables your marriage to be right. Therefore, think seriously about what you allow your mind to dwell on. Philippians 4:8 clearly presents what our priorities should be:

> **"Whatever is true, whatever is noble, whatever is right, whatever is pure, whatever is lovely, whatever is admirable— if anything is excellent or praiseworthy— think about such things."**

WHAT IS the Root Cause of Troubled Marriages?

Jim Dobson recalls in late adulthood a vivid memory that serves as a poignant life lesson.

In his freshman year of high school, young Jim runs a mile race in a field of about 20 athletes and finishes second to a senior who rarely loses. Later, during his sophomore year, his workouts aren't quite as diligent. When he takes off in another race, initially he's in the lead, but then his body becomes wracked with pain and his lungs are desperately sucking in air. Now his desire isn't to win, but merely to collapse on the infield grass, which is exactly what happens. He describes himself as "a sweating heap of shame and failure."[24]

The life lesson, applicable to marriage, is that great beginnings aren't as important as great finishes. Married life is like a marathon—it's important to finish well and honor the marriage commitment. And according to the Bible, we have supernatural power available to help us honor our vows for a lifetime. We need to run the race, focusing on the One who is our strength.

"Therefore, since we are surrounded by such a great cloud of witnesses, let us throw off everything that hinders and the sin that so easily entangles. And let us run with perseverance the race marked out for us, fixing our eyes on Jesus, the pioneer and perfecter of faith. For the joy set before him he endured the cross, scorning its shame, and sat down at the right hand of the throne of God" (Hebrews 12:1–2).

Those who enter marriage with the goal of *getting* rather than *giving* are living with the unrealistic expectation that a spouse can meet their deepest inner needs.

The Three God-Given Inner Needs

In reality, we have all been created with three God-given inner needs: love, significance, and security.[25]

▶ **Love**—to know that someone is unconditionally committed to our best interest

"My command is this: Love each other as I have loved you" (John 15:12).

▶ **Significance**—to know that our lives have meaning and purpose

"I cry out to God Most High, to God who fulfills his purpose for me" (Psalm 57:2 ESV).

▶ **Security**—to feel accepted and a sense of belonging

"Whoever fears the LORD has a secure fortress, and for their children it will be a refuge" (Proverbs 14:26).

The Ultimate Need-Meeter

Why did God give us these deep inner needs, knowing that people and self-effort fail us?

God gave us these inner needs so that we would come to know Him as our Need-Meeter. Our needs are designed by God to draw us into a deeper dependence on Christ. God did not create any person or position or any amount of power or possessions to meet the deepest needs in our lives. If a person or thing could meet all our needs, we wouldn't need God! The Lord will use circumstances and bring positive people into our lives as an extension of His care and compassion, but ultimately only God can satisfy all the needs of our hearts. The Bible says ...

> "The LORD will guide you always;
> he will satisfy your needs in a sun-scorched
> land and will strengthen your frame.
> You will be like a well-watered garden,
> like a spring whose waters never fail."
> (Isaiah 58:11)

The apostle Paul revealed this truth by first asking, *"What a wretched man I am. Who will rescue me from this body that is subject to death?"* He then answers his own question by saying he is saved by *"Jesus Christ our Lord!"* (Romans 7:24–25).

All along, the Lord planned to meet our deepest needs for ...

▶ **Love**—*"I* [the Lord] *have loved you with an everlasting love; I have drawn you with unfailing kindness"* (Jeremiah 31:3).

▶ **Significance**—*"'For I know the plans I have for you,' declares the LORD, 'plans to prosper you and not to harm you, plans to give you hope and a future'"* (Jeremiah 29:11).

▶ **Security**—*"The LORD himself goes before you and will be with you; he will never leave you nor forsake you. Do not be afraid; do not be discouraged"* (Deuteronomy 31:8).

The truth is that our God-given needs for love, significance, and security can be legitimately met in Christ Jesus!

Philippians 4:19 makes it plain:

> "My God will meet all your needs according to the riches of his glory in Christ Jesus."

▶ **WRONG BELIEF:**

"I have the right to expect my marriage partner to meet all my needs."

RIGHT BELIEF:

"God will empower me to keep my marriage commitment. I will look to the Lord to provide my deepest needs and allow Christ to love and serve my mate and others through me."

> "The Son of Man did not come to be served, but to serve, and to give his life as a ransom for many."
> (Matthew 20:28)

Plan of Salvation

FOUR POINTS OF GOD'S PLAN

#1 God's Purpose for You is *Salvation*.

What was God's motivation in sending Jesus Christ to earth?

To express His love for you by saving you!

The Bible says, *"God so loved the world that he gave his one and only Son, that whoever believes in him shall not perish but have eternal life. For God did not* send his Son into the world to condemn the world, but to save the world through him" (John 3:16–17).

What was Jesus' purpose in coming to earth?

To forgive your sins, to empower you to have victory over sin, and to enable you to live a fulfilled life!

Jesus said, *"I have come that they may have life, and that they may have it more abundantly"* (John 10:10 NKJV).

#2 Your Problem is *Sin*.

What exactly is sin?

Sin is living independently of God's standard—knowing what is right, but choosing what is wrong.

The Bible says, *"If anyone, then, knows the good they ought to do and doesn't do it, it is sin for them"* (James 4:17).

What is the major consequence of sin?

Spiritual death, eternal separation from God.

Scripture states, "*Your iniquities* [sins] *have separated you from your God"* (Isaiah 59:2). *"The wages of sin is death, but the gift of God is eternal life in Christ Jesus our Lord"* (Romans 6:23).

#3 God's Provision for You is the *Savior*.

Can anything remove the penalty for sin?

Yes! Jesus died on the cross to personally pay the penalty for your sins.

The Bible says, *"God demonstrates his own love for us in this: While we were still sinners, Christ died for us"* (Romans 5:8).

Belief in (entrusting your life to) Jesus Christ as the only way to God the Father.

Jesus says, *"I am the way and the truth and the life. No one comes to the Father except through me"* (John 14:6). *"Believe in the Lord Jesus, and you will be saved"* (Acts 16:31).

#4 Your Part is *Surrender.*

Give Christ control of your life, entrusting yourself to Him.

"Jesus said to his disciples, 'Whoever wants to be my disciple must deny themselves and take up their cross [die to your own self-rule] *and follow me. For whoever wants to save their life will lose it, but whoever loses their life for me will find it. What good will it be for someone to gain the whole world, yet forfeit their soul?'"* (Matthew 16:24–26).

Place your faith in (rely on) Jesus Christ as your personal Lord and Savior and reject your "good works" as a means of earning God's approval.

"It is by grace you have been saved, through faith—and this is not from yourselves, it is the gift of God—not by works, so that no one can boast" (Ephesians 2:8–9).

The moment you choose to receive Jesus as your Lord and Savior—entrusting your life to Him—He comes to live inside you. Then He gives you His power to live the fulfilled life God has planned for you. If you want to be fully forgiven by God and become the person God created you to be, you can tell Him in a simple, heartfelt prayer like this:

PRAYER OF SALVATION

*"God, I want a real relationship with You.
I admit that many times I've chosen
to go my own way instead of Your way.
Please forgive me for my sins.
Jesus, thank You for dying on the cross
to pay the penalty for my sins.
Come into my life to be
my Lord and my Savior.
Change me from the inside out and make me
the person You created me to be.
In Your holy name I pray. Amen."*

WHAT CAN YOU NOW EXPECT?

If you sincerely prayed this prayer, look at what God says about you!

> "Very truly I tell you, whoever
> hears my word and believes him
> who sent me has eternal life
> and will not be judged but has
> crossed over from death to life."
> (John 5:24)

STEPS TO SOLUTION

Jim and Shirley Dobson display respect and mutual submission in their marriage, but Shirley did not grow up with parents who modeled a godly marriage.

Raised in an alcoholic home, her father slams his fists through walls and spews his threats on her mom. Brown butcher paper and a coat of paint conceal gaping holes in the walls, a temporary fix for a house badly in need of repair. Shirley's family is poor. So often, she wears hand-me-downs two sizes too big.

But thanks to her mother, Shirley finds true wealth. Her mother insists that she go to church, where Shirley accepts Jesus as her Savior and her life is changed forever. Now, she becomes part of God's family. Now, He's charting the course for her life—the unique course that involves a wonderful marriage partner and her participation in powerful, life-impacting ministries.[26]

The principle of *mutual submission* applies to marriage as well as other relationships. We submit to God based on our love for the Lord and our desire to do His will. This is also true in marriage. Because of their love for God, both husband and wife learn to defer to the desires of the other.

KEY VERSE TO MEMORIZE

*"Submit to one another
out of reverence for Christ"*
(Ephesians 5:21).

Key Passage to Read

Dr. James Dobson remains steadfastly committed to being a public spokesman concerning the truth about marriage—that it is designed to be a reflection of the intimate love relationship between Christ and His church. Concerning his radio show *Family Talk*, he commented: "Please don't expect me to take a 'softer, gentler' approach to the issues that burn within my soul. I have never spoken or written without passion for values in which I believe, and I don't intend to start now.

"Babies are dying, the very definition of marriage is under attack, the financial underpinnings of families are being destroyed by confiscatory taxation, and children of all ages are being taught wickedness and every form of godlessness. This is no time to grow timid!"[27]

Clearly, Dr. Dobson takes to heart the exhortation of the apostle Peter:

> "But in your hearts revere Christ as Lord.
> Always be prepared to give
> an answer to everyone who asks you
> to give the reason for the hope
> that you have."
> (1 Peter 3:15)

As Dr. Dobson clearly believes—God designed the marriage relationship to reflect the covenant relationship of Christ and His church. This is the message of Ephesians 5:21–33.

Ancient codes regarding family life often included exhortations for wives and children to obey the head of the family. The apostle Paul, led by the Holy Spirit, approached the topic of family life and relationships from an entirely new and unique perspective. He began by encouraging all people (even husbands) to demonstrate submission, continued by calling for sacrificial love, and concluded by defining submission as a deep and abiding respect. Build a marriage that will last by following the instruction from Ephesians chapter 5.

▶ *"Submit to one another out of reverence for Christ"* (v. 21).

- All believers follow the leadership of Christ and submit to each other.
- At times, a husband submits his desires and interests to the desires of his wife.
- At other times, a wife submits her wishes to those of her husband.

▶ *"Wives, submit yourselves to your own husbands as you do to the Lord. For the husband is the head of the wife as Christ is the head of the church, his body, of which he is the Savior. Now as the church submits to Christ, so also wives should submit to their husbands in everything"* (vv. 22–24).

- Wives respond to their husbands just as the church follows the leadership of Christ.
- Wives listen to and respect their husbands like the church does to Christ.
- Husbands provide and care for their wives like Christ does for His church.

▶ *"Husbands, love your wives, just as Christ loved the church and gave himself up for her to make her holy, cleansing her by the washing with water through the word, and to present her to himself as a radiant church, without stain or wrinkle or any other blemish, but holy and blameless"* (vv. 25–27).

- Husbands serve and provide leadership in the home, just as Christ serves and provides leadership for the church.
- Christ never dominates or forces the church, but rather lovingly serves.
- Husbands are never to berate or abuse their wives, but are to always love and lead.

▶ *"In this same way, husbands ought to love their wives as their own bodies. He who loves his wife loves himself. After all, no one ever hated their own body, but they feed and care for their body, just as Christ does the church—for we are members of his body. 'For this reason a man will leave his father and mother and be united to his wife, and the two will become one flesh'"* (vv. 28–31).

- The physical head protects the other parts of the physical body just as a husband protects and provides for his wife.
- Husbands love their wives unselfishly just as Christ loves the church.
- Husbands and wives share a unique relationship of commitment and care.

▶ *"This is a profound mystery—but I am talking about Christ and the church. However, each one of you also must love his wife as he loves himself, and the wife must respect her husband"* (vv. 32–33).

- The marriage union is a reflection of the relationship between Christ and His bride, the church.
- Mutual respect for their relationship and respective positions and sacrificial love should characterize marriage.
- The marriage relationship is a unique covenant, demanding unqualified commitment to each other.

How to Have a Transformed Life

When it comes to marriage, many couples are missing the mark. Some spouses keep commitments as long as it is convenient—focused on "getting" rather than "giving." They fail to experience the full blessing and beauty of what God intends for marriage—a sustained spiritual union that reflects Christ's unconditional love and sacrifice for the church.

Husbands and wives further miss the mark by striving for a happy marriage in their own strength, relying on emotional reserves that are susceptible to change and depletion. God's strength, however, never falters or fails. He is always available to help godly marriages thrive even in the midst of threatening circumstances.

Couples can consistently reach the target by heeding the insightful call of Scripture:

"Direct me in the path of your commands,
for there I find delight. Turn my heart toward
your statutes and not toward selfish gain."
(Psalm 119:35–36)

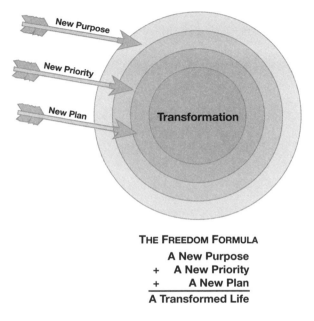

THE FREEDOM FORMULA

	A New Purpose
+	A New Priority
+	A New Plan
	A Transformed Life

Target #1—A New Purpose: God's purpose for me is to be conformed to the character of Christ.

> *"Those God foreknew he also predestined to be conformed to the image of his Son ..."* (Romans 8:29).

- "I'll do whatever it takes to be conformed to the character of Christ."

Target #2—A New Priority: God's priority for me is to change my thinking.

> *"Do not conform to the pattern of this world, but be transformed by the renewing of your mind"* (Romans 12:2).

- "I'll do whatever it takes to line up my thinking with God's thinking.

Target #3—A New Plan: God's plan for me is to rely on Christ's strength, not my strength, to be all He created me to be.

"I can do all things through him who strengthens me" (Philippians 4:13 ESV).

- "I'll do whatever it takes to fulfill His plan in His strength."

My Personalized Plan

"Marriage should be honored by all, and the marriage bed kept pure, for God will judge the adulterer and all the sexually immoral" (Hebrews 13:4).

As I seek to cooperate with God in transforming my marriage, I will ...

▶ **Become** aware of my vulnerability.
- *Realize* that no matter how long I have been married, I am never completely safe from the lure of sin.
- *Resist* the ways of the world.
- *Recognize* the potential lure of a midlife crisis.
- *Refrain* from enmeshed relationships among couples.
- *Review* major events in my life and identify ways that they may have negatively altered my thinking.
  - ▶ children leaving home
  - ▶ severe depression or rejection

- ▶ extended illness
- ▶ class reunions
- ▶ times of bereavement
- ▶ retirement, boredom
- ▶ job losses or changes
- ▶ illness/impairment of a child/grandchild

"The prudent see danger and take refuge, but the simple keep going and pay the penalty" (Proverbs 22:3).

▶ **Guard** the gateway to my mind against inappropriate ...

- ▪ *Television* shows, movies, or music
- ▪ *Topics* that friends and I discuss
- ▪ *Technology* use, websites, texting relationships
- ▪ *Tempting* reading materials
- ▪ *Tantalizing* daydreams and toxic places

"Whatever is true, whatever is noble, whatever is right, whatever is pure, whatever is lovely, whatever is admirable—if anything is excellent or praiseworthy— think about such things" (Philippians 4:8).

▶ **Focus** on building up my mate.

- ▪ *Provide* positive affirmation.
- ▪ *Praise* talents, qualities, and successes.
- ▪ *Perform* acts of kindness.
- ▪ *Practice* unselfish love.

"Encourage one another and build each other up, just as in fact you are doing" (1 Thessalonians 5:11).

▶ **Value** and practice forgiveness.

- *Recognize* my need to be forgiven.
- *Rehearse* these words: "Forgive me, I am sorry."
- *Realize* that love is being able to confess my faults and to forgive the faults of my mate.
- *Release* my right to dwell on my mate's offenses.
- *Remember* that forgiveness is divine and is required of me by God.

"Be kind and compassionate to one another, forgiving each other, just as in Christ God forgave you" (Ephesians 4:32).

▶ **Keep** the lines of communication open.

- *Converse* honestly and sincerely.
- *Communicate* with warmth, genuineness, and empathy.
- *Carefully* watch my body language to make sure it reflects my words.
- *Celebrate* love with both my words and my heart.
- *Concentrate* on what is being said and give feedback on what I hear.

"If I speak in the tongues of men and of angels, but have not love, I am a noisy gong or a clanging cymbal" (1 Corinthians 13:1 ESV).

▶ **Confide** in another committed Christian.

- *Set up* a meeting with my pastor or another mature spiritual leader.
- *Seek* a Christian family counselor.
- *Solicit* advice from a loving, older Christian in my church.
- *Search* for support from someone I trust.
- *Select* a prayer partner to support my marriage.

"Plans fail for lack of counsel, but with many advisers they succeed" (Proverbs 15:22).

▶ **Renew** my commitments.

- *Remember* the feelings I had when I chose my mate and the reasons I made that choice.
- *Reread* my wedding vows out loud—thinking seriously about each one.
- *Reinvite* Jesus into my marriage and home, and talk with Him throughout each day.
- *Recall* the Lord's leading through His Word and the Holy Spirit's gentle guidance.
- *Reaffirm* to the Lord that I am willing to follow His leading.

"Trust in the Lord *with all your heart and lean not on your own understanding; in all your ways submit to him, and he will make your paths straight"* (Proverbs 3:5–6).

Submission is not an act of *weakness*, but a position of *strength*. It is not just for the wife, but it is for both the wife and husband. It is a choice to act on faith, choosing to trust God to work His will through the authorities in your life. As Jesus faced the agony of the cross, His words, *"yet not my will, but yours be done"* (Luke 22:42), demonstrate the strength required for your heart to be fully yielded to God.

As a couple committed to follow Christ's example ...

▶ **Choose to live** under your God-given authorities.

"The authorities that exist have been established by God" (Romans 13:1).

▶ **Choose to pray** for those in authority over you.

"I urge, then, first of all, that petitions, prayers, intercession and thanksgiving be made for all people—for kings and all those in authority, that we may live peaceful and quiet lives in all godliness and holiness" (1 Timothy 2:1–2).

▶ **Choose to respect** the position rather than the personality.

"Let everyone be subject to the governing authorities, for there is no authority except that which God has established" (Romans 13:1).

▶ **Choose to sacrificially submit** to others out of reverence for Christ.

"Walk in the way of love, just as Christ loved us and gave himself up for us as a fragrant offering and sacrifice to God" (Ephesians 5:2).

▶ **Choose to please** others rather than seeking your own way.

"Do nothing out of selfish ambition or vain conceit. Rather, in humility value others above yourselves" (Philippians 2:3).

▶ **Choose to put** your future in the hands of God.

"'I know the plans I have for you,' declares the LORD, 'plans to prosper you and not to harm you, plans to give you hope and a future'" (Jeremiah 29:11).

▶ **Choose to be submissive**, even if it means hardship and suffering.

"... suffering produces perseverance; perseverance, character; and character, hope" (Romans 5:3–4).

▶ **Choose to thank God**, regardless of the end result.

"Give thanks in all circumstances; for this is God's will for you in Christ Jesus" (1 Thessalonians 5:18).

When Not to Submit

QUESTION: "Both the husband and the wife are to submit to one another out of love and reverence for God, but are there times, in addition to when abuse is occurring, when a mate should *not* submit to the desires or demands of a spouse?"

ANSWER: Submission stops at the threshold of violating God's moral principles.

▶ **Do not submit when asked to violate God's Word.**

You are to submit first to God and are never to violate a scriptural command.

"We must obey God rather than men"
(Acts 5:29 ESV).

▶ **Do not submit when asked to violate your conscience.**

Your conscience is God-given, and you should obey it when you are in doubt.

"I will never admit you are in the right; till I die, I will not deny my integrity. I will maintain my innocence and never let go of it; my conscience will not reproach me as long as I live" (Job 27:5–6).

▶ **Do not submit to an action that does not glorify God.**

You are not to engage in deception even though Sarah submitted to Abraham's request to deceive Pharoah and King Abimelech (Genesis 12:10–20; 20:1–10). Abraham and Sarah failed to trust God for their safety. As a result, they were banished from the land and they brought dishonor on their God.

> *"Then Abimelech called Abraham in and said, 'What have you done to us? How have I wronged you that you have brought such great guilt upon me and my kingdom? You have done things to me that should never be done'"* (Genesis 20:9).

When you establish your personal boundaries based on Scripture, never feel that you must submit when pressured to step over into sin.

"Redeem me from man's oppression, that I may keep your precepts" (Psalm 119:134 ESV).

HOW TO Respond to Your Mate's Desires

When Shirley began dating Jim Dobson, she hesitated to tell him about her abusive upbringing, fearing that perhaps he would not accept her or want to deal with the accompanying emotional issues.[28]

But for decades now Dr. Dobson has been allowing Christ to love Shirley through him, nurturing her in the Lord, helping her build Christ-centered worth. Therefore, Shirley has been the recipient of the Lord's extraordinary love—powerful, stabilizing, ever faithful.

> "And I pray that you, being rooted and established in love, may have power, together with all the Lord's holy people, to grasp how wide and long and high and deep is the love of Christ, and to know this love that surpasses knowledge— that you may be filled to the measure

of all the fullness of God."
(Ephesians 3:17–19)

Although everyone has the same three God-given inner needs—the needs for love, significance, and security—God designed the husband to have a greater need for personal significance, while the wife is uniquely created with a deeper need for security. A crucial element in the marriage relationship is becoming aware of your partner's needs and learning to meet them creatively.[29]

The Bible states it this way:

> "Let each of you look not only to his own interests, but also to the interests of others." (Philippians 2:4 ESV)

Wives, Your Husband Desires ...[30]

▶ **Respect**

- *Reaffirm* his positive character traits regularly.
- *Reassure* him of his capabilities.
- *Respect* his burden of responsibility.

"... the wife must respect her husband" (Ephesians 5:33).

▶ **Companionship**

- *Develop* mutual interests that the two of you can share.
- *Discuss* knowledgeably your husband's job and work environment.
- *Determine* to become interested and/or proficient in activities your husband likes.

"'The two will become one flesh.' So they are no longer two, but one ..." (Mark 10:8).

▶ **Household Support**
- *Maintain* a peaceful home atmosphere.
- *Manage* the home efficiently.
- *Maximize* your efforts together to plan for the family's future.

"She watches over the affairs of her household and does not eat the bread of idleness" (Proverbs 31:27).

▶ **Attractiveness**
- *Develop* inner beauty that earns respect.
- *Display* inner strength regardless of outward circumstances.
- *Dress* in an attractively appropriate, feminine manner.

"She is clothed with strength and dignity ... " (Proverbs 31:25).

▶ **Sexual Fulfillment**
- *Be willing* to be a responsive wife.
- *Be willing* to communicate your sexual needs.
- *Be willing* to give assurance that your husband is sexually adequate.

"Her husband has full confidence in her and lacks nothing of value. She brings him good, not harm, all the days of her life" (Proverbs 31:11–12).

▶ **Affection**

- *Tenderly* hug, hold, and kiss her.
- *Tell* her how much you love and care for her.
- *Take* time to learn what speaks love to her and put it into action.

"Husbands, love your wives and do not be harsh with them" (Colossians 3:19).

▶ **Communication**

- *Learn* to share your feelings with her, not just your thoughts.
- *Listen* with concern and interest when she shares her heart with you.
- *Lovingly* encourage her while complimenting her positive character traits.

"Do not let any unwholesome talk come out of your mouths, but only what is helpful for building others up according to their needs, that it may benefit those who listen" (Ephesians 4:29).

▶ **Honesty**

- *Commit* to being totally truthful with her.
- *Confide* in her your true thoughts, feelings, needs, and desires.
- *Communicate* your plans clearly and thoroughly.

"An honest answer is like a kiss on the lips" (Proverbs 24:26).

▶ **Financial Security**

- *Shoulder* financial responsibility for the family.

- *Strategize* with her on how to best use finances.
- *Set* a budget *together* to deal with debt and to plan for the future.

"Anyone who does not provide for their relatives, and especially for their own household, has denied the faith and is worse than an unbeliever" (1 Timothy 5:8).

▶ **Commitment**

- *Seek* to make your wife and family your highest earthly priority.
- *Schedule* quality and quantity time alone with her.
- *Speak* often about your commitment to her.

"Husbands, in the same way be considerate as you live with your wives, and treat them with respect as the weaker partner and as heirs with you of the gracious gift of life, so that nothing will hinder your prayers" (1 Peter 3:7).

As you seek to fulfill the desires of your mate, make a list of ten specific acts you think would please your spouse as an expression of your love.

▶ A wife can show her husband respect by asking for his perspective, opinion, or advice.

▶ A husband can encourage his wife by seeking her insight regarding his friends, business associates, and business activities.

Each week make a plan to practice at least one thing on your list.

> "Dear friends, since God so loved us,
> we also ought to love one another.
> No one has ever seen God; but if we love
> one another, God lives in us
> and his love is made complete in us."
> (1 John 4:11–12)

HOW TO Make the Most of Your Marriage

Because they are in a covenant relationship, Jim and Shirley have committed to never considering divorce as an option for their "differences."

Most people don't realize the devastating effect divorce has on a wide circle of relationships, especially children who are left feeling angry and abandoned. By God's design within marriage, children typically feel nurtured and secure when both parents are present. However, when one parent leaves, one-third of children have what researchers describe as "overwhelming" fear that the other parent will abandon them.[32]

The very heart of marriage is a covenant relationship. Just as God often reaffirmed His covenant with His people, a husband and wife must never lose their covenant commitment to each other. This commitment is not only to your mate, but also to the marriage itself. Commitment goes much deeper than romantic love and empowers you to keep an unbreakable covenant with your marriage partner—regardless of the unexpected circumstances life will bring.

God spoke of His commitment to His people through His prophet Hosea: *"I will betroth you to me forever; I will betroth you in righteousness and justice, in love and compassion. I will betroth you in faithfulness"* (Hosea 2:19–20).

Covenant Checklist

A helpful checklist is found in this acrostic of the word **COVENANT**.

Commit to working through problems, not walking away.

- Agree together that divorce is not an option.

- Agree to communicate feelings and opinions honestly and lovingly.

- Agree to stop and talk when your mate becomes upset or when tension arises between you.

- Agree to understand the reasons for each other's actions.

"Are you pledged to a woman? Do not seek to be released" (1 Corinthians 7:27).

Offer love to your mate even when you don't feel like it.

- Assess how your love compares to that described in 1 Corinthians chapter 13.

  (Substitute your name in the place of the word *love* in verses 4–8.)

- Ask, "Are there times when you feel that I've been impatient and unkind?"

- Ask, "Are there times when you feel that I've not forgiven you?"

- Agree to forgive each other freely, refusing to keep a record of wrongs.

"Love is patient, love is kind. It does not envy, it does not boast, it is not proud. It does not dishonor others, it is not self-seeking, it is not easily angered, it keeps no record of wrongs. Love does not delight in evil but rejoices with the truth. It always protects, always trusts, always hopes, always perseveres. Love never fails" (1 Corinthians 13:4–8).

View your marriage as God's setting for spiritual growth.

- Reveal the needs in your life for love, significance, and security and identify how those needs are presently being met.[33]
- Realize that God did not create any one person to be all you need.
- Rest in the truth that God is your ultimate Need-Meeter, while seeing your mate as God's gift to meet many of your needs, but not all of them.
- Receive your mate's help in discovering and overcoming your blind spots.

"Whoever heeds life-giving correction will be at home among the wise" (Proverbs 15:31).

Eliminate the emphasis on your rights.

- Detect what makes you angry.
- Determine what personal rights you feel have been violated when you become angry.
- Disclose sensitively both the cause of your anger and your honest desires.

"I feel dishonored and unimportant when my

requests are ignored, so it would mean a lot to me if you would take out the trash."

- Decide that once you've expressed your desires, you will yield your rights to the Lord and allow your anger to dissipate.

"Everyone should be quick to listen, slow to speak and slow to become angry, because human anger does not produce the righteousness that God desires" (James 1:19–20).

Nurture your identity in Christ.

- Recognize whether or not your sense of self-worth is based on how your mate treats you.
- Realize that your true worth is based on Christ's dying for you and His living in you (Colossians 1:27).
- Read the New Testament letters and rewrite what it means for you to be *"in Christ"* and to have *"Christ in you."* Example: "I have Christ's strength to do what is right before God." (Read Philippians 4:13.)
- Relax in the truth that your true identity is in Christ, not in your mate.

"I have been crucified with Christ and I no longer live, but Christ lives in me. The life I now live in the body, I live by faith in the Son of God, who loved me and gave himself for me" (Galatians 2:20).

Ask God to change you.

- Ask the Lord to reveal what areas in your life need changing.
- Ask your mate, "Would you name one area in my life where you feel I need the most change?"

- Ask your mate, "Would you help me devise a plan for improvement?"
- Ask God to give you the desire and the power to change.

"Create in me a pure heart, O God, and renew a steadfast spirit within me" (Psalm 51:10).

Nourish your extended family relationships.

- Determine the tangible and emotional needs of your in-laws. Ask yourself, "What acts of kindness can I do that are totally unexpected?"
- Discover your opportunity to draw relatives to Christ through your love.
- Decide to never say unkind words about your mate's family.
- Daily pray for those who have hurt you—forgive and forgive again.

"Honor your father and your mother, so that you may live long in the land the LORD your God is giving you" (Exodus 20:12).

Turn your expectations over to God.

- Talk about the unrealistic expectations you have had of marriage and of your mate.
- Think about how God can bring complete fulfillment to you regardless of your marriage partner.
- Trust that your relationship with God is more important than your relationship with your mate.
- Thank God that He will work in your marriage for your ultimate good.

"Truly my soul finds rest in God; my salvation comes from him. Truly he is my rock and my salvation; he is my fortress, I will never be shaken ... Yes, my soul, find rest in God; my hope comes from him" (Psalm 62:1–2, 5).

HOW TO Apply Do's and Don'ts When Conflict Arises

When vows are spoken at a wedding ceremony, all ears are attuned to hear two people repeat two simple words: "I do." Just as important as those "Do's" are a few "Don'ts"—especially when a couple is in conflict.

> **"Don't have anything to do with foolish and stupid arguments, because you know they produce quarrels."**
> **(2 Timothy 2:23)**

Do's and Don'ts in Marital Conflict

▶ **Don't** offer kind words or gestures with the expectation of receiving the same in return.

Do offer kindness as a free gift with no expectation of return.

"It is more blessed to give than to receive" (Acts 20:35).

▶ **Don't** say, "You always ... " or "You never ... " Extreme accusations or overstatements diminish the impact of a legitimate concern.

Do say, "When I (see or hear …), I feel (hurt, sad, etc.)." Allow statements to speak to your own experience, not phrased as an accusation.

"The hearts of the wise make their mouths prudent, and their lips promote instruction" (Proverbs 16:23).

▶ **Don't** say, "You make me feel … " We have control over our own emotions.

Do take ownership of your own feelings by saying, "I feel … when … "

"The soothing tongue is a tree of life, but a perverse tongue crushes the spirit" (Proverbs 15:4).

▶ **Don't** feel compelled to fix your mate's unresolved concerns.

Do seek to understand why your mate is sharing the situation with you (needing answers, sympathy, companionship, etc.).

"The heart of the discerning acquires knowledge, for the ears of the wise seek it out" (Proverbs 18:15).

▶ **Don't** attempt to resolve recurring issues in the heat of the moment.

Do find a time to calmly discuss an unresolved conflict when there is less tension.

"A hot-tempered person stirs up conflict, but the one who is patient calms a quarrel" (Proverbs 15:18).

▶ **Don't** ignore responsibility for your part in a conflict. Say, "I realize I was wrong when … "

Do take complete ownership of your fault in a conflict, even when it's only 1% of the problem.

"Whoever conceals their sins does not prosper, but the one who confesses and renounces them finds mercy" (Proverbs 28:13).

▶ **Don't** keep score. This only builds resentment and will eventually lead to heated conflict.

Do address one situation at a time, allowing your mate the opportunity to make it right.

"Love ... keeps no record of wrongs"
(1 Corinthians 13:4–5).

▶ **Don't** expect your mate to repeatedly ask forgiveness for the same offense.

Do leave the past in the past and acknowledge your own need to be fully forgiven.

"Bear with each other and forgive one another if any of you has a grievance against someone. Forgive as the Lord forgave you" (Colossians 3:13).

> *Most important in marriage is commitment—the covenant: "Till death do us part." While fortunes change from good to bad and feelings move from up to down, commitment is bedrock for couples. The covenant commitment is solid gold. Commitment is the glue that holds.*
>
> —June Hunt

SCRIPTURES TO MEMORIZE

If I am unhappy in my marriage, is it okay to **separate** even though I know **God has joined** us **together**?

*"What **God has joined together**, let no one separate."* (Mark 10:9)

Is it true that God instructs both husbands and wives to **submit to one another**?

*"**Submit to one another** out of reverence for Christ."* (Ephesians 5:21)

Will my spouse and I be able to **always persevere** if we genuinely **love** each other?

*"**Love** does not delight in evil but rejoices with the truth. It always protects, always trusts, always hopes, **always perseveres**."* (1 Corinthians 13:6–7)

What **is** true, godly **love**?

*"**Love is** patient, love is kind. It does not envy, it does not boast, it is not proud. It does not dishonor others, it is not self-seeking, it is not easily angered, it keeps no record of wrongs."* (1 Corinthians 13:4–5)

Doesn't a husband have authority over his own body, and likewise a wife have authority over her own body?

*"The husband should fulfill his marital duty to his wife, and likewise the wife to her husband. The **wife** does not **have authority over her own body** but yields it to her husband. In the same way, the **husband** does not **have authority over his own body** but yields it to his wife."* (1 Corinthians 7:3–4)

When two people are married, are they to be one in spirit and of one mind?

*"Make my joy complete by being like-minded, having the same love, being **one in spirit** and **of one mind**."* (Philippians 2:2)

Are husbands to love their wives just as Christ loved the church?

*"**Husbands**, **love** your **wives**, **just as Christ loved the church** and gave himself up for her."* (Ephesians 5:25)

In today's society, does God still require wives to submit to their husbands?

*"**Wives**, **submit** yourselves **to** your own **husbands** as you do to the Lord. For the husband is the head of the wife as Christ is the head of the church, his body, of which he is the Savior."* (Ephesians 5:22–23)

Does God expect **husbands** to **be considerate** to their **wives** and to **treat them with respect**?

*"**Husbands**, in the same way **be considerate** as you live with your **wives**, and **treat them with respect** as the weaker partner and as heirs with you of the gracious gift of life, so that nothing will hinder your prayers."* (1 Peter 3:7)

Should **wives submit to** their **own husbands** even if their husbands **do not believe the Word** of God?

*"**Wives**, in the same way **submit** yourselves **to** your **own husbands** so that, if any of them **do not believe the word**, they may be won over without words by the behavior of their wives, when they see the purity and reverence of your lives."* (1 Peter 3:1–2)

NOTES

1. Ruth Bell Graham, *It's My Turn: Life Lessons From the Wife of Billy Graham* (Charlotte, Billy Graham Evangelistic Association, 2007).

2. Gary Thomas, *Sacred-Marriage: What if God Designed Marriage More to Make Us Holy Than to Make Us Happy?* (Grand Rapids, Zondervan, 2000).

3. James Dobson, "Focus on the Family Newsletter—February, 1995," 2.

4. Dobson, "Newsletter—February, 1995," 1.

5. *Merriam-Webster Collegiate Dictionary* (2001), s.v. "Marriage, http://www.m-w.com.

6. Dobson, "Newsletter—February, 1995," 1.

7. W. E. Vine, *Vine's Complete Expository Dictionary of Biblical Words*, electronic ed. (Nashville: Thomas Nelson, 1996); *Merriam-Webster Collegiate Dictionary*.

8. Dobson, "Newsletter—February, 1995," 1.

9. Charles R. Swindoll, *Strike the Original Match* (Portland, OR: Multnomah, 1980), 21–22; Gary R. Collins, *Christian Counseling: A Comprehensive Guide*, rev. ed. (Dallas: Word, 1988), 409; Charles M. Sell, *Achieving the Impossible: Intimate Marriage* (Portland, OR: Multnomah, 1982), 37–39; David Augsburger, *Sustaining Love: Healing & Growth in the Passages of Marriage* (Ventura, CA: Regal, 1988), 186–187.

10. Dobson, "Newsletter—February, 1995," 2.

11. Dobson, "Newsletter—February, 1995," 2.

12. *Merriam-Webster,* s.v. "Monogamy."

13. *Merriam-Webster,* s.v. "Polygamy."

14. Dobson, "Real Love: Vive la Difference" (Colorado Springs, CO: Family Talk, 1995), http://www.drjamesdobson.org/real-love/vive-la-difference.

15. Dobson, "Real Love: Vive la Difference."

16. Dobson, "Real Love: Vive la Difference."

17. James Dobson, *Love for a Lifetime* (Colorado Springs, CO: Multnomah Books, 1998), 57–58.

18. Dobson, *Love for a Lifetime*, 58.

19. Dobson, *Love for a Lifetime*, 79.

20. Dobson, *Love for a Lifetime*, 80.

21. Lawrence J. Crabb, Jr., *The Marriage Builder: A Blueprint for Couples and Counselors* (Grand Rapids: Zondervan, 1982), 29–30.

22. Dobson, *Love for a Lifetime*, 51.

23. Dobson, *Love for a Lifetime*, 52.

24. Dobson, *Love for a Lifetime*, 119.

25. Lawrence J. Crabb, Jr., *Understanding People: Deep Longings for Relationship*, Ministry Resources Library (Grand Rapids: Zondervan, 1987), 15–16; Robert S. McGee, *The Search for Significance*, 2nd ed. (Houston, TX: Rapha, 1990), 27–30.

26. James Dobson, Shirley Dobson, *Night Light: A Devotional for Couples* (Carol Stream, IL: Tyndale, 2008), "January 28."

27. Tobin Grant, "Political Advocacy Tracker: Dobson and Dobson," *Christianity Today* May 2010, http://www.christianitytoday.com/ct/2010/mayweb-only/28-51.0.html.

28. Dobson and Dobson, *Night Light*, "January 28."

29. Crabb, Jr., *The Marriage Builder,* 33–34.

30. Willard F. Harley, Jr. *His Needs, Her Needs: Building an Affair-Proof Marriage*, 15th Anniversary ed. (Grand Rapids: Fleming H. Revell, 2001), 183–184.

31. Harley, Jr. *His Needs, Her Needs*, 182–183.

32. James Dobson, *Building a Marriage that Lasts* (Colorado Springs, CO: Family Talk, 2011), 3.

33. Crabb, Jr., *Understanding People*, 15–16; McGee, *The Search for Significance*, 2nd ed., 27–30.

June Hunt's HOPE FOR THE HEART minibooks are biblically-based, and full of practical advice that is relevant, spiritually-fulfilling and wholesome.

HOPE FOR THE HEART TITLES

www.aspirepress.com

The HOPE FOR THE HEART
Biblical Counseling Library
is Your Solution!

- Easy-to-read, perfect for anyone.
- Short. Only 96 pages. Good for the busy person.
- Christ-centered biblical advice and practical help
- Tested and proven over 20 years of June Hunt's radio ministry
- 30 titles in the series – each tackling a key issue people face today.
- Affordable. You or your church can give away, lend, or sell them.

Display available for churches and ministries.

www.aspirepress.com